Yvonne Morgan-McKenzie was born in Yallahs, Jamaica in the West Indies. Always a hard worker; she helped her mother, Olga Morgan, a lot with cooking and cleaning. Later in life she worked in the Cayman Islands first as a cook in restaurants then as a nanny where she helped with raising five children.

As time went by, she eventually moved to New York where she did training to care for elderly people. Yvonne never forgot her roots and spent lots of time cooking. She was always trying different recipes for which "coconut" was a main ingredient.

In loving memory of the greatest woman My Mother, Olga Adassa Morgan, you taught me all about hard work and perseverance.

Yvonne Morgan-McKenzie

COCONUT 100 WAYS

AUSTIN MACAULEY PUBLISHERS™

LONDON • CAMBRIDGE • NEW YORK • SHARJAH

A CIP catalogue record for this title is available from the British Library.

ISBN 9781398496064 (Paperback)
ISBN 9781398496071 (Hardback)
ISBN 9781398496088 (ePub e-book)

www.austinmacauley.com

First Published 2023
Austin Macauley Publishers Ltd®
1 Canada Square
Canary Wharf
London
E14 5AA

To Brenda Wood Tatum who has helped me with getting this project off the ground by contacting the publishers on my behalf and all the other secretarial things that I'm too busy cooking to do.

Foreword

Growing up in the countryside of Jamaica with a Rastafarian brother, coconut was a must in almost every meal. My late mother Olga Adassa also adored this fruit. Many days coconut was our "meat". Coconut oil becomes medicine and when needed, mixed with other ingredients to suit the complaint at the time. It is also used as hair oil or lotion. The husk was a floor brush and the shell was a dish, cup or hair clip or used as a flower pot for our orchid.

Cooking abbreviations	Unit of measurement
c	cup
t	teaspoon
T	tablespoon
lb	pound
oz	ounce
gal	gallon
pk	peck

Jamaican Original Seasonings

Jerk Seasoning

Scotch Bonnet Peppers
Scallion
Thyme
Onion
Pimento
Garlic
Rosemary
Nutmeg

Pepper Elder

Ginger
Vanilla Beans
Black Pepper
Lemon
Vinegar
Molasses
Annatto Seeds

Green Blend

Thyme
Scotch Bonnet de-seeded
Ginger
Onion
Garlic
All-purpose seasoning
Vinegar

Jamaican Jerk Pork Seasoning

1 bottle beer (Red Stripe or other Lager)
4 guava leaves
½ onion
½ c ginger
½ c scallion
4 green pepper leaves
10 pimento seeds
8 cloves garlic
½ c coconut oil
6 scotch bonnet peppers – de-seeded

Method

Wash and blend until smooth. Store in a clean tight jar.

Jamaican Made Seafood Gravy

1 lb shrimp heads
1 lb fish head
5 t salt
1 t black pepper
1 stick butter
2 t flour
Thyme, scotch bonnet de-seeded, garlic
Large onion
½ c orange juice
2 T coconut oil
Pimento seeds/leaves

Method

Add coconut coil oil to a pot, heat, add onion, thyme, salt, fish and shrimp heads.

Toss for five minutes then add the rest of the ingredients. Cover with water and boil for 15 minutes. Mix flour in cold water, add it and boil for three minutes.

Strain and cool. Save in fridge until needed.

Coconut Oil

6 dry coconuts
Water for squeezing

Method

Crack coconuts and warm shell on flame so that the flesh is removed easily. Cut into small pieces and blend. Strain coconut and water into a bowl. Set overnight so the milk will come to the top. This must be skimmed with a cup to another pot to form oil when boiled all the way down to oil.

Sweet & Sour Sauce

1 c mango
3 c pineapple
Onion
1 c ketchup
Vinegar
2 carrots
½ c guava jam, ginger thyme, pimento seeds, scotch bonnet
pepper de-seeded
1 T salt
½ c brown sugar
2 T corn starch
½ c orange juice
Thyme
Ginger
Garlic
1 c coconut milk
Bell pepper – red and green

Method

Peel vegetables, cut into one-inch lengths. Save pineapple
skin to make a broth.

Pressure-cook pineapple skin, onion, scallion, thyme, ginger, garlic and sweet pepper until tender. Strain off the liquid. Add ketchup, guava jam, corn starch mixed in coconut milk.

In a pot, add 2 t oil, 1 c carrot, ½ onion, 1 c pineapple, ½ of each bell pepper.

Add to the meat of choice and boil until thick.

Porridges

Almond and Green Banana Porridge

1 c almonds
2 green bananas
2 t flour
Coconut milk
Spices – nutmeg and vanilla
Sweetening – condensed milk or sugar and honey

Method

In a blender, add cut bananas and coconut milk. Blend until smooth.
In a two quart pot, boil two cups water and spices.
Add flour, mix well then add the banana and almond mixture.
Cook for 10 minutes on medium flame.
Turn off the heat. Sweeten with condensed milk or sugar and honey.

Jamaica Made Easy Oat Porridge

2 c raw oats
5 c coconut milk
½ c brown sugar
1 can condensed milk
Spices – nutmeg
Cinnamon leaves/stick

Method

In a pot, add oats and water as directed on the package. Bring to a boil. This will double the oats.

Add spices and coconut milk. Stir and boil for 10 minutes. Sweeten with sugar or condensed milk, if necessary. Add salt and vanilla to taste. Additional spices if required.

Jamaican Made Easy Taste Oats with Banana

2 c raw oats
1 ripe banana
5 T coconut milk
Brown sugar
1 can condensed milk
Nutmeg
Cinnamon sticks or leaves
Salt
Vanilla

Method

Place oats in a pot and cover with water. Bring to a boil. This will double the oats.

Add spices, coconut milk and banana. Stir. Bring to a boil and cook for 10 minutes. Sweeten, if necessary.

Add salt and vanilla to taste. Extra spices may be added to taste.

Jamaican Coco Porridge "Baby"

2 c coco
1 c sugar
3 T flour
1 T vanilla
1 t salt
1 nutmeg
1 t cinnamon leaves
3 c coconut milk

Method

Peel coco. Cut, cook and blend with coconut milk. In a pot, bring to boil cinnamon leaves. Add cocoa, flour and spices. Boil until creamy to make a nice porridge. Sweeten with sugar.

Add milk of your choice – baby formula or Lasco milk for babies.

Aphrodisiacs

Jamaican Jelly – Front End Lifter

Cow foot
Cow skin
Syrup
Salt
Spice – Rum, red syrup, almond, nutmeg, condensed milk, 2 t ginger juice, 2 t coconut milk

Method

Cook until tender – approximately 2 hours
Strain with a cloth.
Add spices and mix.
Put in fridge to gel.

Jamaican Made Chicken Foot Jelly

2 lbs chicken feet
2 cucumbers
½ c lime juice
½ c vinegar
2 t sea salt
Black pepper
1 c onion

Method

Wash and clean chicken feet. Cook until tender.
Cool. Strain liquid from the pot to make jelly.
In a bowl, clean and cut vegetables. Add chicken feet and other ingredients.
Best after 24 hours.

Jamaican Style Pig Foot Jelly

3 lbs pig feet
1 c lime juice
2 t sea salt
10 pimento seeds
Onions/scallion
Scotch bonnet de-seeded for taste

Method

Clean pig feet well. In a pot of boiling water, add pig feet and boil until a weblike substance covers the top of the water. Remove this and discard this. Cover with water, lime juice, salt and seasonings. Cook until tender. Cool and debone. Cut the pig feet flesh into small pieces. In a bowl, add meat and cover with juice from the pot. Place in fridge overnight to set.

Oysters in Coconut Sauce

24 oysters covered with coconut milk

Thyme

Onion

2 garlic cloves

2 fish seasoning

Method

In a pot combine all ingredients and boil for 20 minutes.

Turtle and Smoked Meat

3 lbs turtle meat
2 lbs smoke meat
2 t green seasoning
2 t jerk seasoning
1 c chipped carrot
1 c chipped potatoes
Thyme
2 beef cubes
Salt, pepper, scallion
2 t coconut oil
Pimento leaves
½ c coconut milk and flour for spinners (dumplings)

Method

In a big pot with pimento leaves, pepper and meat, cover with water and boil for 10 minutes to clean first. Drain water.

In a pressure cooker, heat coconut oil, add turtle, smoked meat and half of the seasoning. Cover with hot water and pressure cook for 40 minutes. Open the pot and add remaining seasoning and vegetables. Pressure cook for 30 minutes. Open the pot and stir. Add dumplings and cook for 10 minutes over medium flame.

Serve with rice or other starch as desired.

Cracked Conch

2½ lbs conch cleaned
2 eggs
½ c cream (evaporated milk)
Sea salt
Black pepper
½ c flour
Lime
Tartar sauce
Coconut oil

Method

Pound conch until tender. Cut into 1-inch pieces.
In a bowl, mix eggs, cream, salt and flour. Dip conch in the liquid and coat each piece well with flour.
In a large pan, heat oil.
Cook strips until brown and drain on a paper towel lined plate.
Serve with tartar sauce or cocktail sauce and a squeeze of lime.
Serve with French fries.

Conch in Coconut
Milk with Dumplings

4 large conch cleaned
2 cans coconut milk
Salt and pepper
Butter
1 c flour
Water

Method

Pound conch until thin, cut into 1-inch pieces. Season with salt and pepper and fry in a pan with butter until lightly brown. To the pot with conch, add coconut milk and boil. Then reduce heat and simmer for 20 minutes.

Mix flour and water until tacky. Knead and when done, roll out the dough and make long dumplings. Add to conch in a pan and cook for 15 minutes.

Serve with rice.

Conch and Coconut Rice

2 lbs conch, jerk seasoning

3 c rice

Scotch bonnet pepper de-seed, bell peppers – red, green, yellow

Onion, thyme, scallion

4 c coconut milk

2 fish cubes

1 t salt

Black pepper

Method

Cut conch in thin strips and season with jerk seasoning.

In a pot, fry conch. Add coconut milk and other seasoning finely chopped.

Bring to a boil, add rice, cook for 10 minutes then add bell pepper and fish cubes.

Stir well and simmer for 15 minutes.

Marinated Conch

3 lbs conch, cleaned and tenderized
1 c ketchup
Juice of a large lime
1 small onion finely cut
½ green bell pepper finely cut
Scallion
½ scotch bonnet pepper de-seeded and minced
2 t pick-a-peppa sauce

Method

In a large bowl, combine all ingredients until well mixed.
Serve with crackers.

Conch Fritters

3 lbs cleaned conch, tenderized
1 green bell pepper finely chopped
1 small onion finely chopped
2 eggs
1 t salt
1 t black pepper
1 scotch bonnet pepper deseeded
1 c flour
Milk

Method

In a food processor, chop conch, onion and peppers (chopped coarsely).
Mix the remaining ingredients to hold the mixture together.
Heat oil in a deep frying pan. Add balls of the mixture and fry until golden brown.
Serve with tartar sauce or cocktail sauce.

Conch Fritters with Beer

1 lb conch (cleaned and cut finely)
Coconut oil
Onions
Scotch bonnet pepper
Garlic
Flour
2 t baking powder
Maggi fish seasoning

Method

In a bowl, add seasoning to conch. Add flour using beer to make a batter. Set aside to allow flavours to develop before frying.
In hot coconut oil, fry conch fritters until golden brown.
Serve with tartar or cocktail sauce.

Jamaican Goat Head Soup

Goat head

Carrot

2 c yams

2 c pumpkin

1 cho cho

Carrots

Green bananas

Dasheen

4 cloves garlic

Pimento leaves

Seasoning: scallion, thyme, 4 t sea salt, black pepper, scotch bonnet peppers (green and ripe)

Method

Scrape and burn goat head. Cut and clean well.

In a pressure cooker, cover goat head with water and add garlic and pimento leaves. Pressure cook for 40 minutes.

Wash and cut all breadkind. In a soup pot, boil cut food and boil goat for one hour. Add hot water. Mix flour in a bowl with salt and water to make "spinners" – long small dumplings).

Add all the seasoning to taste.

Add a mannish water noodle packet if needed.

Jamaican Cow Cod Stew

Seasonings – green blend, jerk blend, pimento seed, 2 t salt, scotch bonnet pepper

2 lbs cleaned cow cod

2 lbs pumpkin

1 c coconut milk

2 t coconut oil

Garlic

Bell pepper

Carrot

1 c mix flour

Ginger

Packet pumpkin soup mix

Cornmeal

Maggi vegetable seasoning

Method

In a pressure cooker, heat oil and half the seasoning then add cow cod. Cook until tender (for 20 minutes). Add coconut milk, vegetable seasoning, tomato, pumpkin soup mix and cook for another 20 minutes. Mix flour and water to make spinners (long dumplings). Cook 15 more minutes and add more seasoning, if necessary.

Serve with rice or other starch.

Drinks

Pina Colada Mix

1 15.5 oz can crushed pineapple
1 46 oz can pineapple juice
1 can evaporated milk
1 can cream of coconut

Method

Blend ingredients until smooth. Pour into a large bottle and store in fridge.

For virgin pina coladas

Shake and mix well. Pour over crushed ice in a blender. Blend until smooth

For real pina coladas

Shake and mix well. Pour the mixture over crushed ice in a blender. Add 1–2 shots of coconut rum and blend until smooth

Both can be served in a hurricane glass with an umbrella, ½ slice of orange and a cherry.

Carrot Punch

1 lb carrots
Beetroot
1 can condensed milk
Brown sugar
Vanilla
Ground nutmeg
Cinnamon
½ c rum

Method

Boil carrot and beetroot until tender. Blend until smooth. Add spices, condensed milk and rum. Also add one bottle of Guinness.
Serve with ice.

Jamaica Breadfruit Punch

½ ripe breadfruit
1 can condensed milk
1 t salt
2 t nutmeg
1 t cinnamon
2 t vanilla
¼ c brown sugar
1 bottle dragon stout

Method

Peel, gut, cut and wash breadfruit.

In a pot cover with water and boil for 10 minutes. Cover with water and cook for 15 minutes. Add more water in the same pot to cover breadfruit.

Blend fruit with all water in pot. Pour in a jug. Sweeten with condensed milk, add spices and dragon Stout.

June Plum Juice

1 dozen plums deseeded
¼ ginger
2 lbs sugar
2 limes

Method

Wash and blend plums and ginger. Strain, sweeten and add lime
Serve over ice.

Homemade Fruit Punch

1 46-oz can pineapple juice

1 46-oz can orange juice

½ c grenadine or strawberry syrup

Method

Mix well and store in a bottle in the fridge.

Can be served as regular fruit punch over ice.

Or

For rum punch – add 1 shot of gold rum per 8 oz serving over ice.

Jamaican Style Tropical Punch

1 large ripe mango
2 passion fruit
1 ripe plantain
1 beetroot
1 gal water
½ lb sugar
1 ¼ of a ginger root (boiled and strained)

Method

Wash and peel fruits. Cut and blend until creamy. Sweeten and serve with ice.

Sea Moss

½ lb sea moss
½ t nutmeg
½ t cumin
1 c coconut milk
1 c sugar
1 can condensed milk
½ c rum
2 t vanilla

Method

Clean and wash sea moss. Boil in a pressure cooker for 30 minutes.
Add coconut milk and set aside to cool. Add all the spices. Sweeten to taste.
Serve with ice.

Cucumber (Cool Cat) Drink

3 large cucumbers
1 lb sugar
2 limes
¼ t ginger
1 gal water

Method

Wash and cut cucumbers and ginger. Liquefy in a blender. Strain.
Add mixture to water and lime and sweeten with sugar.
Serve with ice.

Jamaican Sorrel Drink

3 c sorrel fruits
¼ lb ginger
4 cinnamon leaves or sticks
Pimento seeds or leaves
Brown sugar
White rum
Red label wine

Method

Wash, cut and blend ginger. In a large pot, add sorrel, ginger, cinnamon leaves and pimento.
Cover with water and bring to a boil. Turn off the flame.
Cover. Let sit overnight and then strain. Sweeten to taste.
Add rum and wine.
Serve with ice.

Jamaica Fruit Smoothie

½ c mango
2 ripe bananas
½ c coconut milk
Brown sugar
½ c pineapple
1 c ice
Spices – ½ t nutmeg

Method

Wash, clean and cut fruits.
In a blender, add coconut milk, banana, mango then pineapple ice and spices.
Blend until smooth.

Jamaica Ginger Beer

1 lb fresh ginger
2 lbs brown sugar
6 limes
1 gal water

Method

Wash and blend ginger. In a large pot, add water and ginger and boil for 10 minutes. Turn off then add lime juice and skin of 3 limes. Boil again for 10 minutes. Strain and sweeten. Serve over ice.

Sour Sop Juice

One large soursop
2 limes
Ginger
Brown sugar
Nutmeg
Vanilla
Water

Method

Wash fruit. Add to blender and pulse to extract juice. Add ginger and blend mixture.
Strain, sweeten to taste. Add lime and spice.

Guava Juice

1 dozen guavas
¼ t ginger
1 c sugar
1 gal water
1 lime

Method

Wash and blend guava and ginger. Add sugar and lime.
Serve over ice.

Papaya and Banana Smoothie

1 lb papaya
4 ripe bananas
4 c water
2 t honey

Method

Wash papaya. Spoon seeds out and cut into pieces. Combine bananas, papaya, water, honey and 2 c ice.
Blend well.

Mains

Party Size Honey Mustard Chicken or Pork

25 lbs chicken parts and pork shoulder cut and cleaned
6 t green seasoning
1 c honey
1½ c mustard
3 t salt
Black pepper
3 scotch bonnet peppers
1 c garlic chopped
1 pk coconut butter

Method

Blend all the seasoning and pour over chicken/pork mixture. Mix well and set overnight.
Bring to room temperature and bake at 350 degrees for 35 minutes. Turn meat over and bake for another 25 minutes.

Sweet & Sour Chicken

3 lbs cut-up chicken

Dry batter – 1 t salt

Garlic

1 c flour

Coconut oil

Sweet & sour sauce

1 c mango

3 c pineapple

Onion

1 c ketchup

2 carrots

½ c guava jam, ginger thyme, pimento seeds, scotch bonnet pepper de-seeded

1 t salt

½ c brown sugar

2 t corn starch

½ c orange juice

Thyme

Ginger

Garlic

1 c coconut milk

Bell pepper – red and green

Method

Wash and cut the chicken into small pieces. Season with dry batter and fry for 10 minutes in coconut oil.

Peel vegetables and cut them into one-inch lengths. Save pineapple skin to make a broth.

Sauce

Pressure cook pineapple skin, onion, scallion, thyme, ginger, garlic and sweet pepper until tender. Strain off liquid. Add ketchup, guava jam, corn starch mix in coconut milk.

In a pot, add 2 t oil, 1 c carrot, ½ onion, 1 c pineapple, ½ of each bell pepper

Add fried chicken and liquid juice – ketchup, jam, corn starch. Mix with coconut milk. Boil until thickened.

Serve with rice or other starch.

Stuffed Pot Roast

4 lbs beef
Green blend and jerk blend
Slice garlic, cut onion, scallion
2 beef bouillon cube
½ c red label wine
Coconut oil

Method

Cut holes in beef one inch apart. Stuff mixed seasoning in these. Rest in the fridge overnight for three days.
Let beef come to room temperature.
Heat coconut oil on medium flame. Add meat and turn every 10 minutes until tender.
Add 1 t of hot water, if necessary.
Serve with rice or other starch.

Pressure Cooker Stew Beef

2 lbs beef
Garlic
Onion
Thyme
Scotch bonnet pepper
6 pimento seeds, blended
2 t coconut oil
1 carrot
1 potato
1 t browning
1 beef bouillon cube

Method

Clean and cut beef and vegetables. Season well. Marinate overnight.

Heat oil in a pressure cooker, add beef and stir. Add 1 c water and pressure for 15 minutes. Cool and open and add all remaining ingredients. Pressure cook for five minutes. Cool and open. Stir while cooking for five minutes. Add more hot water, if necessary.

Serve with rice or other starch.

Oxtail and Ribs

2 lbs oxtail cut and trimmed

2 lbs ribs

Garlic, onion, scallion, scotch bonnet pepper, pimento seed/leaves

1 c potatoes

2 t coconut oil

Green blend

Vinegar, lime, 2 beef bouillon cubes

2 t corn starch

Method

Wash and trim meat.

Season meat well and let marinate overnight.

On a baking tray, place meat and bake at 350 degrees for two hours.

In a pot with coconut oil, stir vegetables and season to release flavour, then add meat. Cover half with hot water and cubes. Cook till tender.

Stir in corn starch and mix well. Cook for five minutes.

Serve with rice or other starch.

Jamaica Breadfruit, Coconut, Salt Mackerel

1 salted mackerel
1 breadfruit
3 c coconut milk
Onion, scallion, thyme, scotch bonnet pepper – deseeded,
Tomatoes, pimento leaves

Method

Peel and slice breadfruit.
In a pot, boil mackerel, clean and set aside.
In another pot, place breadfruit slices, cover with coconut milk and bring to a boil. After 10 minutes, add all the seasoning and cook. Add salt mackerel and cook for additional five minutes.
Serve with rice or other starch.

Salt Mackerel Rundown

Salt mackerel
2 tomatoes
Scotch bonnet pepper
Onion
Bell pepper
Thyme
Scallion
1 peg garlic
Coconut milk
1 t curry powder (optional)

Method

Soak mackerel overnight to desalt or bring to a boil twice x four minutes with fresh water each time.
Clean and debone.
In a saucepan, boil coconut milk for 10 minutes then add all the seasoning. Boil for another 10 minutes, add mackerel and sea salt, if necessary.
Serve with rice or other starch.

Salt Fish Flitters

2 c flour
1 c cleaned and picked saltfish
Scotch bonnet pepper de-seeded
1 egg
1 onion
Coconut oil to fry

Method

Cut onion and pepper finely. Beat egg. Mix all ingredients into flour.
In a hot frying pan with coconut oil, spoon and fry batter until golden brown.

Jamaican Oxtail Stew

4 lbs oxtail
1½ small tomatoes
2 t salt
1 c onion
Scotch bonnet pepper
Broad beans
Seasoning – garlic, ginger, thyme, pimento
Coconut milk
2 t coconut oil

Method

Soak broad beans overnight. Season meat with blender seasoning. Rub in thyme and pimento. Add onion after.

In a pressure cooker, add oxtail, garlic and ginger. Cook for 40 minutes. Cool and open the pressure cooker, add beans and season with tomato, onions, coconut milk and coconut oil. Pressure cook for another 20 minutes. Cool and open. Add salt and browning, if required, for taste.

Serve with rice or other starch.

Pepper Steak

2 lbs beef
Bell peppers (red, yellow, green)
2 t jerk season sauce
1 large onion
½ c flour
1 t corn starch
Coconut milk
Garlic
Ginger
1 carrot
½ c coconut oil
½ t corn starch

Method

Clean beef and cut it into strips. Cut vegetables in equal strips
Flour and fry beef in a pot with coconut oil for three minutes.
Set aside.
Cook vegetables for two minutes then mix jerk sauce and corn
starch in coconut milk. Combine all ingredients and cook for
four minutes, stirring constantly.
Serve with rice or other starch.

Jamaican Baked Chicken

4 lbs leg quarters
Jerk seasoning
Green blend
3 t sugar
Sea salt
Black pepper
Coconut oil
Chicken bouillon cube

Method

Wash and cut leg quarters in half. In a bowl, combine jerk season and green blend.
Marinate overnight.
Bake at 350 degrees for one hour.
Serve with rice or other starch.

Jamaican Callaloo and Salt Fish

1 lb callaloo
1 c salt fish washed and deboned
Onion
Scallion
Tomatoes
Scotch bonnet pepper
Coconut oil
2 t coconut milk
2 t butter

Method

Strip the fresh callaloo and cut fine. Add seasoning
Add oil to pot. Fry fish then add vegetables. Heat pot and add
oil. Fry fish then add vegetables.
Cook on medium heat for three minutes, add callaloo and
steam for five minutes.
Serve with cassava bammy.

Jamaican Curry Shrimp

2 lbs shrimp
1 t salt
Black pepper
2 t onion
2 t garlic
2 t jerk seasoning
Ginger
Thyme
Scallion
Scotch bonnet de-seeded
2 t coconut oil
2 t butter
1 c coconut milk in curry

Method

In a saucepan, sauté oil, curry and butter. Add shrimp and cook for three minutes. Remove shrimp from pan. Add seasonings and coconut milk. Cook for eight minutes. Add shrimp to sauce.
Serve with rice.

Jamaican Made Lemon Lobster

2 whole lobsters
1 c orange juice
Onion
Thyme
Scotch bonnet pepper
Bell peppers – red, yellow and green
Scallion
1 c butter
½ lemon
2 t coconut oil
2 t salt
Black pepper

Method

Wash and clean lobsters, season and cut in equal sizes.
In a sauce pot, on medium heat, add oil and butter. Add garlic rub, salt, and black pepper to lobster. While cooking, continue to pour liquid over lobster. Cover and cook for five minutes. Remove the lid and add all the remaining seasoning. Cook on medium flame for five minutes. Turn the flame off. Lobster will continue to cook when the flame is off.
Serve with rice or other starch.

Jamaican Made Oven Baked Jerk Chicken Wings

4 lbs chicken wings
2 t sea salt, ginger
2 t fresh garlic
2 limes squeezed
2 t brown sugar
Jerk season blend
Coconut oil for brushing

Method

Clean and dry wings. In a sauce pan, add 1 t oil and brown sugar, burn to make browning.
Season wings. Set to one side for best result.
Place wings on baking sheet in oven that has been preheated to 375 degrees then brush with juice from wings.
Cook for 45 minutes.

Jamaican Made Pork Shoulder

5 lbs pork shoulder

Scotch bonnet pepper

Mango jelly

Pineapple slices

Pimento seeds

Orange juice

Scallion

Thyme

Onion

½ c salt

Cloves

Ginger

Jerk blend

Green blend

Method

Wash pork using the brining method. Cook pork in brine for one hour. Remove from brine and cut slits in pork to apply extra topping. Blend Seasonings. Stuff in holes.

Rub Jerk Blend and mango jelly over pork. Bake in oven for 1½ hours at 275 degrees. Remove from the oven and baste with juice from Pork. Add pineapple slices and broil in the oven for five minutes. Serve with rice or other starch.

Jamaican Steam Cabbage and Saltfish

1 3-lb cabbage
½ lb salt fish
½ lb small tomatoes
1 onion
2 t oil
Scotch bonnet to taste
Bell pepper

Method

Wash cabbage. Shred as small as possible.

Place salt fish in a pot and cover with cold water. Boil for 10 minutes. Pour off cooking water. Refill with fresh water and re-boil for 10 minutes. Pour off water then clean and de-bone.

Clean, cut and wash the vegetables and season. In a pot, heat oil, add fish and fry for two minutes. Add cabbage and other seasoning. Steam on medium heat for 10 minutes.

Serve with rice or other starch.

Jamaican Salt Fish Casserole

1 lb saltfish
2 c yellow yam
2 c cheese
2 t onion
Tomato
Bell pepper
Garlic
Scotch bonnet pepper
Thyme
Scallion
1 lime/orange

Method

Cook and crush yam. Boil salt fish twice with fresh water each time to cover. Drain, clean and pick saltfish. Cut clean vegetables.

In a casserole dish, make layers – yam, salt fish, seasonings, cheese. Repeat for next layers.

Add orange then cheese on top.

Bake at 350 degrees for 40 minutes.

Jamaican Steam Fish and Vegetables

4 medium fish
Onion
Scallion
Irish potatoes
Pimento seed/leaves
Vinegar
Pumpkin
1 carrot
Fish tea mix
1 c butter
Okra
Coconut oil
Coconut milk

Method

Clean and de-bone fish. Dry.

In a sauce pan, heat oil on medium flame. Add half of fish tea mix. Brown for two minutes, add fish and the remaining ingredients. Steam for 15 minutes.

Serve with rice or other starch.

Jamaican String Beans with Carrot and Pumpkin

1 lb string beans
1 lb carrots
1 lb pumpkin
2 t butter
1 t salt
Black pepper
Onion
Garlic

Method

Clean and cut the vegetables lengthwise. Add all the ingredients in a pot. Bring to a boil and cook on low flame for 10 minutes.

Jamaican Baked Lamb and Carrots

4 lbs lamb
2 t jerk season
2 t green blend
1 c flour
Rosemary, thyme
1 onion
3 t garlic
½ c ketchup
3 c carrots

Method

Wash lamb with lime and vinegar. Cut lamb and season well.
Marinate overnight. Bring to room temperature.
On a baking tray, add lamb and season. Bake for 1 hour at 350
degrees.
Serve with roasted potatoes.

Jamaican Reggae Pasta

1 lb tri-colour pasta

2 c cheese

2 eggs

2 t jerk blend

¼ c bread crumbs

½ c butter

½ c flour

Onion

2 t garlic

Method

Boil pasta in a large pot for 10 minutes and drain. In a bowl, beat eggs and add to pasta. In a sauce pan, heat butter, flour. Lightly brown flour and add chopped onions. Add milk to cheese to make a roux. Mix pasta and jerk sauce. In a baking dish, add pasta, seasoning, grated cheese and roux. Sprinkle bread crumbs on top. Cook for 30 minutes at 350 degree.

Jamaica Authentic Escovitch Fish

4 lbs fish

1 c flour

2 c coconut oil

1 c shredded cho cho

2 t sugar

1 c shredded carrots

3 t salt

Black pepper

10 pimento seeds

2 scotch bonnet peppers

Bell peppers – green and red (1 c each)

2 large onions

2 c vinegar

Method

Wash and clean fish – dry.

Crush black pepper grains and pimento seeds. Rub some on fish along with salt.

In a frying pan, heat oil, flour and fry fish dry.

Topping – In a sauce pan, add vegetables which should be cut lengthwise in equal lengths. Balance of seasoning, vinegar, 4 t oil from fish in the same pot. Bring to a boil. Cover and salt to taste.

Serve fish with topping.

Jamaican Stew Peas and Beef

2½ c large red kidney beans
2 lbs salt beef
1 lb fresh beef
4 cloves garlic
Black pepper
3 stalks scallion
Thyme
Pimento seeds
Scotch bonnet pepper
½ c flour
1 c coconut milk
4 black peppercorns

Method

Cut meat into small pieces. Wash salt beef and then boil for 10 minutes to reduce salt content. Add red beans to pressure cooker and cover with water. Bring to a boil for beans to swell and get colour. Add meat and half of cut-up seasoning. Cover with water and ½ c coconut milk. Pressure for 35 minutes. Open and add remaining seasoning and small dumplings (made from remaining coconut milk and flour). Cook for additional 10 minutes.

Serve with rice or other starch.

Oven Roasted Stuffed Pork

6 lbs pork
Jerk blend, green blend
Pepper
Garlic
Onion
Thyme

Method

Dry meat. Cut holes and stuff seasoning into holes. Rub meat well. Leave in fridge up to three days before cooking. Cover in foil and bake at 350 degrees until tender.
Serve with rice or other starch.

Callaloo Omelet

4 eggs

2 c flour

1 c chopped onion

2 c callaloo (cleaned and cut small)

Salt to taste

Black pepper

½ scotch bonnet pepper

1 c chopped tomatoes

1 c red and yellow bell pepper

3 t coconut oil

Method

In a bowl, beat eggs. Combine all the ingredients to make a batter.

In a large frying pan, warm 2 t coconut oil and pour all the batter. Cook for five minutes. Remove cooked mixture to a plate, add 1 t coconut oil and return batter to cook on other side for five minutes.

Thin Beef Easy

1 lb beef
Garlic
Black pepper
Salt
½ t corn starch
½ onion cut finely
2 t jerk sauce – scotch bonnet pepper – deseeded, red label wine, ketchup
¼ c coconut oil

Method

Cut beef in thin slices.
Heat oil. Coat beef in corn starch and fry until golden brown. Remove from pan.
Add onions and pepper to oil stir for three minutes. Mix wine and ketchup and jerk mix. Stir all the ingredients in a pot for two minutes.
Serve with rice or other starch.

Stew Beef Easy

2 lbs stew cut and trimmed
Green blend – thyme, scotch bonnet deseeded, ginger, onion, garlic, all-purpose seasoning, vinegar
Browning
1 carrot
1 potato
Coconut butter
Beef bouillon cube

Method

Season beef with green blend. Brown beef in a hot pot to release flavour. In a pressure cooker, cook for 30 minutes. Cool and open pot, add two cups hot water and fresh seasonings. Cook for additional 15 minutes. Stir to make gravy.
Serve with rice or other starch.

Easy Steamed Fish

Fish – sliced or whole
Scallion
Okra
Onion
Thyme
Scotch bonnet pepper
Bell peppers
Pumpkin
Fish cubes
Pimento seeds
Vinegar
Coconut butter

Method

Clean and season fish well.
Cut vegetables into small pieces.
In a large pot, add all ingredients. Cover and cook on medium
flame for 15 minutes.
Serve with rice or other starch.

Jamaican Steam Cabbage and Saltfish

1 3-lb cabbage
½ lb salt fish
½ lb small tomatoes
1 onion
2 t oil
Scotch bonnet to taste
Bell pepper

Method

Wash cabbage. Shred as small as possible.

Place salt fish in a pot and cover with cold water. Boil for 10 minutes. Pour off cooking water. Refill with fresh water and re-boil for 10 minutes. Pour off water then clean and debone.

Clean, cut and wash vegetables and season. In a pot, heat oil, add fish and fry for two minutes. Add cabbage and other seasoning. Steam on medium heat for 10 minutes.

Serve with rice or other starch.

Jerk Shrimp

2 lb shrimp
2 t jerk seasoning
1 pk coconut
1 t onion powder
½ c coconut
1 t garlic powder
1 t ginger powder
Scallion
Basil
Thyme
1 t corn starch

Method

Clean shrimp and season. In a sauce pan, fry shrimp in butter. Fry for three minutes from each side. Make a gravy w/ coconut milk, corn starch. Bring to a boil. Add shrimp, Maggi cube season.
Serve with rice or other starch.

Shrimp and Garlic

2 lbs shrimp cleaned

1 c finely chopped garlic

1 scotch bonnet pepper

2 t coconut oil

1 fish bouillon cube

4 leaves elder pepper

Method

In a hot pot, add shrimp and all the ingredients in oil. Cover
and cook for five minutes.

Serve with rice or other starch.

Turtle Stew

4 lbs turtle meat
3 t green blend
3 t jerk blend
1 t salt
Black pepper
Vinegar
Coconut oil
Onion
Scallion
Thyme

Method

Clean turtle and season. Let sit overnight in fridge.

In a hot pot with coconut oil, put all meat to brown and develop flavour. After 10 minutes, put into a baking pan with all the seasoning. Cover with foil and bake turtle until tender. Serve with rice or other starch.

Jamaican Made Pepper Shrimp

Coconut butter
2 lb shrimp
Lime
Thyme
Elder pepper leaves
Onions
Pimento leaves and seeds
Garlic
1 t salt
½ t black pepper
Scotch bonnet pepper
Red food colour
Coconut oil
1 Maggi cube

Method

Blend all the seasoning and add food colour.
In a sauce pan, add 2 t oil on medium flame. Then add all the
ingredients. Stir and cook for 10 minutes.
Serve with rice or other starch.

Whole Chicken Easy

1 4-lb chicken
Vinegar
Green blend
Jerk blend
½ c coconut oil

Method

Clean chicken, split back. Season inside out, set overnight for best result.
Brown chicken on medium flame for eight minutes each side until chicken is cooked.
Serve with rice or other starch.

Coconut Pumpkin Rice

2 c rice
2 c pumpkin – diced and cooked
2 c coconut milk
1 t salt

Method

In a pot, bring coconut milk to a boil, add the remaining ingredients. Cook over medium flame for 25 minutes.

KFC Salad

2 c shredded cabbage
1 c shredded carrot
½ c coconut milk
½ c sugar
½ c finely cut onion
1 t white vinegar
¼ t orange juice

Method

In a bowl, wash vegetables, drain well. Combine with coconut
milk, sugar, lime juice, orange juice and vinegar.

Cornmeal Dumplings

1 lb plain flour
½ lb cornmeal
1 t salt
2 c water
1 c coconut milk

Method

Mix flour, cornmeal and salt. Gradually, add some water to form a dough. Knead and set aside for 10 minutes.
Bring a pot with water and coconut milk to a boil. Add salt.
Cut dough as desired and cook in water/coconut milk mixture until done.

Curry Chicken

3 t curry powder
3 lbs chicken
Lime juice
Jerk seasoning
3 t chopped onion
2 t coconut oil
Thyme
Bouillon cubes
Garlic
2 t coconut oil
Scallion
4 pimento seeds
Scotch bonnet pepper
1 cho cho
¼ t black pepper
Sea salt
Corn starch/masala

Method

Wash chicken with lime and cut into one-inch pieces. Peel and cut cho cho into two-inch pieces. Rub all the chicken with jerk seasoning.

In a hot pot, add 2 t coconut oil and 2 t curry, garlic and onion. Stir for two minutes.

Cook chicken on medium flame, stir and add rest of the curry and onion. Cook for 20 minutes in open pot. Mix corn starch in water and pour mixture into chicken.

Cook for an additional four minutes. Turn off the stove.

Serve with white or brown rice.

Jamaica Guava Glazed Salmon

1 lb salmon fillets
½ c guava jam
½ t sea salt
1 lime
Black pepper
2 t coconut oil
1 t butter

Method

Wash and dry salmon. Coat with salt and pepper.
Heat butter and coconut oil in frying pan. Fry fish skin side down.
While cooking, mix lime and jam. Brush on fish and cook for five minutes.
Serve with rice or other starch.

Bulgur Wheat

1 lb bulgur wheat
½ c coconut milk
Sea salt
2 c water

Method

Wash bulgur wheat. Add all ingredients together. Cover with
2 inches of water. Cook for 40 minutes over medium heat.
Goes well with your favourite protein.

Jamaican Vegetable Soup

2 lbs pumpkin
2 ears corn cut in small pieces
2 carrots
1 cho cho
1 c yellow yam
4 potatoes
2 cloves garlic
Scallion
1 c flour
Sea salt
Black pepper
Thyme
Pumpkin soup mix

Method

In a soup pot, boil vegetables for 30 minutes, add flour and seasonings. Bring to a boil again for an hour to make a creamy tasting soup.

Desserts

Guava Cake

Ginger
½ c coconut oil
2 c ripe guava
2 c flour
1 c ginger juice
2 eggs/rind of lime
1 ½ c brown sugar
1 t baking power
½ t baking soda

Method

In a large bowl, combine sugar, oil, eggs, lime rind. Blend guava with ginger juice and add to other ingredients. Fold in flour, baking powder and baking soda.

Pour the mixture into a greased pan and back at 350 degrees for 40 minutes.

Coconut Upside Down Cake

2 c coconut flakes

2 c sugar

4 eggs

3 c all-purpose flour

3 t baking powder

2 c coconut oil

Spices – nutmeg, 1 t cinnamon, 2 t vanilla, 1 c rum, 1 c cut cherries, 1 c raisin

Method

In a saucepan, heat ½ c sugar and 2 t water to caramelize. Stir and set aside to cool.

Grease a baking tin, add caramel, coconut flakes and ½ of cut cherries.

Mix sugar, eggs, rum vanilla and oil until sugar is melted. Add flour and spices then pour the mixture on top of the ingredients in the baking tin.

Bake at 350 degrees for 45 minutes.

Vegan Rum Coconut Cake

Coconut butter

1 c coconut milk

2 c sugar

Nutmeg

Cumin

All spice

½ t salt

3 c flour

Vanilla

4 t baking powder

Bread crumbs

Flax seeds

Spices

Soaked fruits

Rum

Wine

Raisins

Currants

Prunes

Red label wine

Browning as needed

Zest dry orange peel

Method

In a bowl, sift dry ingredients. Heat butter and sugar with fruits. Stir. Turn off heat and mix until the sugar is dissolved. I slowly combine my ingredients mixing, cutting and folding until my spoon is slowly falling.

Bake in greased pan at 350 degrees for 1 hour 20 minutes or until the knife comes out clean.

Jamaican Guava Jelly

24 ripe guavas
2 lbs sugar
2 limes
Water
Cinnamon leaves

Method

In a pot, boil fruits with water for 20 minutes. Strain and use liquid only. Add lime juice which brings out the pectin. Add 1 c sugar per 1 c juice. Boil for 20 minutes or test in a glass of cold water. When jelly goes down in a ball, it is ready. Pour in a clean jar and store.

Jamaican Bun Made Easy

Dry ingredients
3 lbs flour
1½ c sugar
1 t cinnamon
2 c fruit
1 t nutmeg
1 t salt

Wet ingredients
1 c grated coconut
2 eggs
1 bottle stout
4 t butter
Lime
2 t ginger
2 t baking powder
Red label wine

Method

Combine wet ingredients in a bowl, mix well. In a pot, warm stout, fruit, butter, vanilla, spices, salt and eggs. Mix flour and sugar and stir in baking powder. Add to the wet mixture. Mix well.

Pour into greased baking tins.

Bake at 300 degrees for 50 minutes. Brush with honey.

Jamaica Ginger Cheesecake Bars

6 oz ginger cake
¼ c melted butter
8 oz cream cheese
1 can condensed milk
1 egg
½ t nutmeg

Method

In a bowl, mix ginger cake with butter. In another bowl, beat cream cheese. Stir in condensed milk, nutmeg and egg.
Place half of the ginger cake crumble in a baking pan. Press this down with a cup, then add the milk mixture to crumble.
Spread a balance of crumble on top to make a sandwich.
Bake at 375 degrees for 20 minutes.
Let cool, cut and enjoy.

Jamaica Fruit Salad

1 c coconut

1 c local apple

1 c pineapple

1 c mango, papaya and orange

1 ripe banana

Method

In a bowl, cut all fruits in squares. Mix and chill in fridge.

Jamaican Made Plantain Flitter

1 ripe plantain
2 c flour
1 t baking power
1 c sugar
Nutmeg
½ t salt
½ c coconut milk
Coconut oil for frying

Method

Combine dry ingredients in a bowl. Blend plantain with milk and sugar, add spices and vanilla. Combine all the ingredients to make a batter.

Heat coconut oil in a frying pan and fry the batter over medium flame until golden brown.

Jamaican Made Plantain Loaf

1 ripe plantain
2 c + 1 c flour
½ c brown sugar
Nutmeg
1 t + 1 t for dusting
2 t butter
½ t salt
1 t baking power
2 t coconut oil – to brush

Method

In a bowl combine flour, baking powder and salt. Cut in butter and mix with cold water to make dough. Set aside
In a pot, add mashed plantain, sugar, spice 1 t butter. Cook for five minutes then cool.
Roll the dough flat. Fold four times and roll flat again. Use a cup to cut shapes, lay half of these on baking sheet. Spoon plantain mixture on top of dough circles, top with remaining dough. Seal with a fork.
Bake for 25 minutes at 300 degrees.

Jamaican Red Beetroot Cake

2 c flour
1 t baking powder
1 c sugar
½ c milk
½ c coconut oil
½ t salt
1 c beet root
2 eggs

Method

Blend all ingredients except flour. Add to the flour in a bowl.
Bake at 350 degrees for 45 minutes.

Jamaican Made Tropical Bars

2 c white chocolate chips
1 c mango (dehydrated)
1½ cans condensed milk
2 c peanuts finely chopped
1 c almonds
1 c pineapple (dehydrated)
½ c butter
1 c shredded toasted coconut
1 c toasted bulla or ginger bread

Method

In a baking dish, mix 1 c ginger bread/bulla and butter. Use a cup to press this down into the dish.

Mix all ingredients together and press down in the baking dish.

Bake at 375 degrees for 20 minutes.

Cool and cut into bars.

Jamaican Ginger Bulla

½ t ginger
1 c sugar
½ c molasses
1 t salt
1 c cold water
2 t baking powder
2 c flour
Topping
5 t butter

Method

Preheat oven to 350 degrees.
Mix all ingredients together. Add flour until firm.
Roll on a floured surface until flattened (about ½ inch).
Cut out the mixture in circles using a cup or glass.
Grease baking sheet and place bulla mixture on this.
Bake for 25 minutes. When done, brush top of bulla with butter.

Jamaican Plain Bulla

4 c flour

2 c brown sugar

1 t salt

2 t molasses

2 t nutmeg

2 t vanilla

2 t coconut oil

2 t baking powder

½ c butter

Method

In a bowl, rub flour and butter together then add sugar, salt, baking powder and spices to make a dough. Set aside, cover with a wet towel to keep moist for 30 minutes.

On a clean surface, roll dough flat. Cut out shapes with a cup. Bake in preheated oven for 30 minutes at 300 degrees.

Jamaican Hard Dough Bread

½ c coconut milk

1 c oats

3 c flour

2 t instant yeast

1½ t sea salt

3 t sugar

3 t butter

5 oz warm milk

Method

In a bowl, mix dry ingredients. Work butter into the flour mixture and gradually add milk and mix well.

Place dough on a clean board and knead until it becomes elastic.

Place in a large greased bowl. Move dough around bowl until the surface is greased.

Cover with a damp towel and leave to rise for 45 minutes.

Place dough on a lightly floured surface and punch it down to remove air.

Roll out dough in a rectangle.

Tightly roll dough up and make a loaf with it. Place in a greased pan and leave to rise for another 30 minutes.

Bake in a preheated oven for 30 minutes or until top is brown.
Cool for five minutes then place on a rack for further cooling.

Jamaican Cassava Bammy

4 c cassava
1 c coconut milk
2 t coconut oil
Salt to taste

Method

Grate cassava and in a white cheesecloth, strain juice by adding water. Set liquid aside to get starch at the bottom.

In a bowl, rub cassava between your fingers until it is dry. Add salt.

Heat pot then add cassava flour to shape in a ring, press down. Cook over medium heat for 10 minutes. Brush with coconut oil before turning. Cook for another 10 minutes.

Jamaican Made Oat Bread with Honey

2 c flour
2 c oats
½ c honey
1 c grated coconut
1 t salt
2 t coconut milk
½ c butter
2 yeast packets
1 t baking powder
2 eggs
Spices – nutmeg, cinnamon and almond

Method

In a bowl, rub butter in flour. Place yeast in warm water. Mix wet ingredients into dry ingredients. Set for two hours.
Knead dough and form in a bun shape (a long bun). Brush dough with coconut oil.
Bake at 350 degrees for 35 minutes.

Jamaican Soaked Fruits

Dry orange peel
Nutmeg
White rum
Red label wine
Raisin
Cinnamon sticks
Mixed fruits
Currants

Method

In a glass bottle, put all dried fruits and spices. Cover with wine and rum.

Additional rum can be added after 3 months.

Coconut Butter Cookie

1 c grated coconut
1 c sugar
1 egg
1 c coconut butter
½ t almond flour
2 c all-purpose flour

Method

Cream butter, sugar and add beaten eggs. Add the mixture of almond flour and all-purpose flour.

Mix well.

Roll out the mixture on a floured surface and cut cookies.

Grease baking sheet and place cookies on the same.

Bake at 350 degrees for 10 minutes. Let it cool.

To To

2 c flour

3 eggs

Nutmeg

Salt

½ t baking powder

½ t baking soda

6 oz butter

1 c milk

2 c coconut

2 t sugar

1 t vanilla

Method

In a bowl, mix all ingredients. Place on a greased tin and bake for 50 minutes at 350 degrees.

Jamaican Guava Jam

2½ lbs ripe guavas
2 lbs sugar
2 limes
Cinnamon leaves
Water

Method

Cover guava with water and add cinnamon leaves. Boil until soft. Rub fruit with the back of a spoon in a sieve to deseed. Using juice from the pot to strain. Get all seeds out. In a clean pot, measure one cup of sugar to one cup of guava pulp and juice, add lime and boil rapidly for 20 minutes. Store in a jar.

Coconut Donuts

3 c flour
1½ c sugar
4 eggs
1 t salt
1 pk coconut milk
3 t baking powder
1 c water
1 t vanilla
3 c coconut oil for frying

Method

In a bowl, mix eggs, flour and sugar until fluffy. Add salt, coconut milk powder, baking powder and water.
Add vanilla and mix well. Shape and fry in coconut oil. Drain on towel-lined plate.

Cassava Pone

Banana leaves
2 lbs cassava grated
1½ c brown sugar
Softened butter
1 c coconut grated
Nutmeg, cinnamon, vanilla
1 t salt

Method

In a bowl, add all ingredients and mix well.
Warm the banana leaves over open flame. Cut into pieces.
Boil water in a pot. Place mix on banana leaves and wrap.
Drop "packages" in boiling water to cook for at least 10–12 minutes.

Lightning Source UK Ltd.
Milton Keynes UK
UKHW020224220223
417433UK00010B/24